Choir

Gurpreet Kaur Bhatti

I0141053

methuen | drama

LONDON • NEW YORK • OXFORD • NEW DELHI • SYDNEY

METHUEN DRAMA

Bloomsbury Publishing Plc, 50 Bedford Square, London, WC1B 3DP, UK
Bloomsbury Publishing Inc, 1359 Broadway, New York, NY 10018, USA
Bloomsbury Publishing Ireland, 29 Earlsfort Terrace, Dublin 2,
D02 AY28, Ireland

BLOOMSBURY, METHUEN DRAMA and the Methuen
Drama logo are trademarks of Bloomsbury Publishing Plc.

First published in Great Britain 2025

Copyright © Gurpreet Kaur Bhatti, 2025

Gurpreet Kaur Bhatti has asserted their right under the Copyright,
Designs and Patents Act, 1988, to be identified as Author of this work.

Cover image © Bob King Creative for Chichester Festival Theatre

Photograph by Seamus Ryan

All rights reserved. No part of this publication may be: i) reproduced or
transmitted in any form, electronic or mechanical, including photocopying,
recording or by means of any information storage or retrieval system without
prior permission in writing from the publishers; or ii) used or reproduced in
any way for the training, development or operation of artificial intelligence (AI)
technologies, including generative AI technologies. The rights holders
expressly reserve this publication from the text and data mining exception as
per Article 4(3) of the Digital Single Market Directive (EU) 2019/790.

Bloomsbury Publishing Plc does not have any control over, or responsibility
for, any third-party websites referred to or in this book. All internet addresses
given in this book were correct at the time of going to press. The author and
publisher regret any inconvenience caused if addresses have changed or sites
have ceased to exist, but can accept no responsibility for any such changes.

No rights in incidental music or songs contained in the work are hereby
granted and performance rights for any performance/presentation
whatsoever must be obtained from the respective copyright owners.

All rights whatsoever in this play are strictly reserved and application
for performance etc. should be made before rehearsals begin to 42 M&P,
Palladium House, 7th Floor, 1–4 Argyll Street, London, W1F 7TA.
No performance may be given unless a licence has been obtained.

A catalogue record for this book is available from the British Library.

Library of Congress Control Number: 2025943253

ISBN: PB: 978-1-3505-8868-4
ePDF: 978-1-3505-8869-1
eBook: 978-1-3505-8870-7

Series: Modern Plays

Typeset by Mark Heslington Ltd, Scarborough, North Yorkshire

For product safety related questions contact
productsafety@bloomsbury.com.

To find out more about our authors and books visit
www.bloomsbury.com and sign up for our newsletters.

Choir

By **Gurpreet Kaur Bhatti**

The world premiere performance of *Choir* took place at Chichester Festival Theatre's Minerva Theatre on 2 August 2025 with the following cast (in order of speaking):

Morgan	**Laura Checkley**
Ken	**Timothy Speyer**
Anna	**Danusia Samal**
Joy	**Alison Fitzjohn**
Esther	**Danielle Henry**
Paul	**James Gillan**
Sheila	**Annie Wensak**
Freddie	**Keenan Munn-Francis**
TV Runners	**Hannah Dickinson, Maya Williams, Ruby Woodhead**
Director	**Hannah Joss**
Designer	**Anisha Fields**
Music & Sound Designer	**Alexandra Faye Braithwaite**
Lighting Designer	**Jai Morjaria**
Movement Director	**Annie-Lunnette Deakin-Foster**
Music Arranger	**Rich Forbes**
Musical Director & additional arrangements	**Michael Henry**
Casting Director	**Jacob Sparrow**
Voice & Dialect Coach	**Simon Money**
Assistant Director	**Nathanael Campbell**
Production Manager	**Jacqui Leigh**
Costume Supervisor	**Megan Rarity**
Props Supervisors	**Lisa Buckley**
	Tegan Cutts
Company Stage Manager	**Alison Rankin**
Deputy Stage Manager	**Gareth Newcombe**
Assistant Stage Manager	**Rebecca Natalini**

chichester
festival
theatre

Chichester Festival Theatre creates inspiring experiences
that bring people together – on and off the stage. Creativity
is at the heart of everything we do, and we aim to light a
spark in everyone who experiences our work – locally,
regionally, nationally and internationally.

As one of the UK's flagship theatres, we are renowned for
the exceptionally high standard of our productions and our
industry-leading work with the community and young
people. Situated in a cathedral city in West Sussex between
the South Downs and the sea, the Festival Theatre's bold
thrust stage design makes it one of England's most striking
playhouses – equally suited to epic drama and musicals. The
studio theatre, the Minerva, is particularly noted for
premieres of new work alongside intimate revivals. Our new
third venue, The Nest, opened in summer 2025: a vibrant
space for dynamic work and the talent of tomorrow.

Countless productions which started life at CFT have
transferred to the West End or toured nationally and
internationally over the past six decades, from musicals to
significant new plays and classic revivals.

Our Learning, Education and Participation (LEAP)
department works with people of all ages and abilities,
offering a pioneering range of initiatives that inspire and
delight all those who take part.

To read more about us, visit cft.org.uk.

THANKS TO

Justin Audibert and Kathy Bourne for believing in this play

Hannah Joss for her ingenious mind and for making me laugh

Roxana Silbert for being there at the start

Cathy King and Alex Bloch for their constant support and encouragement

Rich and Keeley Forbes for starting something special

The back row altos, past and present, and the entire R Voices Choir for the inspiration and love

Choir

For Margaret

Characters

Morgan
Esther
Joy
Ken
Anna
Paul
Sheila
Freddie

Location

The back room of a suburban pub.

Note

The songs are only suggestions, they can be changed as required.

Scene One – Monday

Curtain/darkness. A stunning solo male voice singing the first line of Queen's 'Somebody to Love'.

Lights up to reveal it's **Paul**.

Morgan *manages the music on a laptop. It blares out via a couple of huge speakers.*

The room comprises a vast floor space with a small stage and signs for the Exit and the Toilets. A few chairs are arranged in sections of twos. This is where the choir sit.

There is a large canvas placed to the side, whatever is on it remains unseen by the audience.

Morgan *conducts the singers (everyone except* **Sheila** *and* **Freddie**) *as they join in the rest of the song with* **Paul**.

Using song sheets, the choir are disengaged and lacklustre. **Morgan** *stops the music.*

Morgan   Getting there. Really . . . almost . . . getting there. Perhaps invest a bit more . . . from your souls . . .

She sings a line from the song.

Morgan   Imagine being utterly desperate to find another human body to offer affection to.

The group eye one another uneasily.

Morgan   And pour that desperation into the words.

Ken   What words?

Morgan   The ones you're singing. Let yourselves be taken over by the music.

Anna   As if we're possessed?

Joy   By Satan?

Morgan   Just give it . . . whatever you've got.

Esther   Sure.

Joy   Okay.

Ken   I'll do my best.

She turns to **Joy** *and* **Esther**.

Morgan   Altos, think of your second line as a . . . a . . . plea to God.

Esther   God. Right, yeah . . . God.

Joy   You mean . . . God from church.

Morgan   Well . . .

Joy   I don't like churches. Strange things happen in churches.

Morgan   Doesn't have to be religious.

Anna   It does say Lord.

Paul   That's just a word.

Joy   Lord Jesus, the Lord is my shepherd, Lord of the Rings . . .

Morgan   Lord in this context represents anything on a higher plane. It could be . . . the sun or the moon.

Joy   Nah, I don't do all that.

Esther   I sort of see what you're getting at.

Morgan   Excellent, Esther. (*To* **Joy**.) How about nature?

Joy   Like trees?

Morgan   Exactly!

Joy (*nods*)   Trees. Trees . . . Trees.

Morgan   Anna . . . that was a beautiful flourish over the top of the bridge. But it does need more lift!

Anna   Lift?

Morgan   Yeah.

Anna   Sort of . . .

She sings with more verve.

Morgan   Er . . .

She sings again with too much vigour.

Morgan   Bring it down a tad.

Anna   I'll find the level when Sheila's here.

Morgan   Where is Sheila?

Esther   She was going to the shops to buy cutlery.

Joy   I didn't know Sheila needed new cutlery.

Anna   Neither did I.

Ken   She's a dark horse.

Morgan   Remember why we're doing this performance. It really really matters. Try and connect with that simple thought. And let's insert big feelings into those lyrics. Massive feelings . . .

She plays the music again. They start to sing. Strangely, **Ken** *falls to his feet as though he's praying/talking in tongues.*

Confused, **Morgan** *stops the music.*

Morgan   Ken, what . . . what?

Ken   I'm showing the torment from my desperation.

Morgan   Our goal is to entertain. Not cause trauma. I think everyone's getting slightly . . .

Anna   Slightly?

Morgan   Overwhelmed. I appreciate this is your first show in front of an audience . . .

Paul   It is not my first show.

Morgan   I mean everyone else. Honestly, you're all capable of sounding . . . as good as . . . any other members of society.

Suddenly **Sheila** *flies in on roller skates. She can't control herself and launches straight into the choir, knocking a couple of them over.*

Sheila *skids all over the place, bumping into things.*

Sheila   I tied the laces too tight, I can't get them off.

Esther   Come here.

She helps her sit down and starts undoing the laces.

Morgan   You're very late, Sheila.

Sheila   Sorry.

Anna   I didn't know you could roller skate.

Sheila   I can't, I found them in the park.

Paul   What park?

Sheila (*thinking quickly*)   Oh actually, no . . . it wasn't the park . . . it was . . . they were in Morrisons by the Free From section . . . I took them to the till but they said they don't sell roller skates. So I asked where the Lost Property was but they don't have Lost Property in Morrisons . . . I waited ages and then the rageful people who work nights came . . . and threatened me with legal action unless I left the premises . . . So I decided to bring them home and then I thought you could use them for your charity, Anna.

Anna   We protect otters.

Sheila   They might not fit.

Esther *manages to take them off.*

Esther   Give them to a school or something.

Sheila *shakes her head.*

Sheila   The teachers'll start asking for my passport and my library card. And I can't think where that is. I'll just have to hold onto them for a while.

The others start to mess about with the roller skates.

Paul   Did you get your cutlery?

Sheila (*shakes her head*)   They were selling them in fours. I only wanted a teaspoon.

Esther   One teaspoon?

Morgan (*loud*)   No more lateness this week! You might not be professionals but you can choose to approach your work with professionalism.

The others are doing a silly trick on the skates. Someone's doing a handstand. They are laughing and not listening to **Morgan**.

Morgan   One more time, please!

They gather, she conducts and they sing 'Somebody to Love'. It's not bad.

Morgan   Better. Marginally better. Take a break and don't forget Freddie's joining us shortly, he's not naturally front-footed so let's make him feel welcome. After he arrives, I've got a special announcement.

Ken   What's that then?

Morgan   Patience, Ken.

Esther   Are you pregnant?

Morgan   No.

Joy   She's too old to be pregnant. Anyway, she hasn't got anyone to get pregnant by.

Esther   She might have gone on Tinder and had a one-night stand.

Joy   Or that *Guardian* Blind Date. They give you a free dinner. And it's not a shit dinner either.

Esther   Sounds alright, having a nice dinner and getting pregnant. Well done you!

Morgan   I'm not pregnant.

Ken   I'll get the drinks.

Morgan   Go easy.

Anna   I sound much better when I'm tipsy.

Morgan   I'm not sure that's true.

Sheila   I'd like to be tipsy.

Paul   What's stopping you?

Sheila   Alcohol makes me urinate. A lot.

Anna   I thought *water* made you urinate.

Sheila   I wish it did. My bladder's a bit wrong. And my sphincter.

Ken (*to* **Sheila**)   What about lager?

Sheila   That's the worst.

Ken   Gin?

Morgan (*interrupts*)   She said alcohol, Ken. Means it's all alcohol.

Ken *exits. The others check their songsheets/phones or stretch out.* **Esther** *and* **Joy** *start painting the canvas.*

Paul *approaches* **Morgan** *in a space where they can't be heard by the others.*

Paul   What's going on?

Morgan   I should tell everyone together.

Paul   I . . . saw James last night. He's coming on Saturday.

Morgan   Oh . . . so it's all . . .

Paul   Yeah.

Morgan   Is he actually going to . . .

Paul   That's what he's saying.

Morgan   As long as he doesn't mess you about again.

Paul   He doesn't mess me about.

Morgan   You said he blocked you the other week.

Paul   Because I threw my flat white in his face . . .

Morgan   Because he asked the barista for his number.

Paul   Only because they used to do Tae Kwondo together.

Morgan   Tae Kwondo?

Paul   I know! He unblocked me . . . after I turned up at his office with a knife.

Morgan   What?

Paul   It was only a butter knife. After I held it to my throat, he explained everything.

Morgan   Can't wait to meet him.

Paul   Don't say anything.

Morgan   About what?

Paul   Anything I've said that . . . you know . . . involves him. When you see him, make it seem like the first time you've heard me mention his name.

Morgan   He's all you ever talk about.

Paul   Are you my best friend or do you want me to die, Morgan?

Morgan   Paul . . .

Paul   I want it to look like . . . I don't care about anybody or anything.

Morgan   I will be perfect. Don't worry, Saturday's going to be amazing.

Paul   I'm not worried.

Morgan   Good.

Paul   Are you worried?

Morgan   Do I look worried?

Paul   Yes.

Anna *is watching* **Esther** *and* **Joy** *painting.*

Anna   Morgan, this is really taking shape.

Morgan *approaches.* **Anna** *points to something.*

Anna   Is that a river?

Joy   No. (*A beat.*) It's a moustache.

Esther   I told her it should be black or at least brown.

Joy   When I think of him, I see him with a blue moustache.

Esther   That doesn't make sense.

Morgan   Freddie hasn't actually got a moustache.

Joy   Won't matter if it's blue then, will it?

Ken (*off*)   Help me, please! Help!

Paul *goes out to* **Ken**. **Sheila** *takes out a Greggs carrier bag.*

Sheila   Anyone fancy a vegan sausage roll?

They gravitate towards **Sheila** *and take a sausage roll.*

Sheila   I made them in front of *Bake Off*.

Esther   Did they do vegan sausage rolls on *Bake Off*?

Sheila   No.

They eat the sausage rolls.

Anna   What's inside?

Sheila (*a beat*)   Vegan.

Esther   These are good, Sheila.

Sheila   How good are they?

Ken *and* **Paul** *bring in drinks and hand them out.*

Esther   Delicious.

Sheila   Are they the best you've ever eaten?

Esther   Er, I'm not sure.

Sheila   Don't worry, I'll never make them again.

Esther   Sheila, they're nice, I just don't think about sausage rolls being the best.

Sheila   What do you think about then?

Paul *and* **Ken** *take sausage rolls.*

Esther   I don't know.

Sheila   There's nowt so queer as folk.

Anna *shows* **Morgan** *a sheet of paper.* **Paul** *peers over her shoulder.*

Anna   And this is definitely the final set list?

Morgan   Yes.

Paul   No Whitney?

Morgan   Stop it.

Joy   I love that woman more than a crack baby loves a rock.

Anna   I think I love her more than my children.

Esther   Please, let us!

Morgan   This choir does not sing Whitney. Not while I'm of sound mind.

Morgan *goes to her laptop, starts organising the music.*

Esther   Oh God, I just got a . . . funny quiver going through my body.

Ken   I'm having those all the time, when I'm at the bus stop, when I'm putting my pants on the radiators, when I'm picking off bits of skin from the back of my heel . . .

Morgan   Nerves are part of the process.

Joy   What if I shit myself?

Morgan   You won't.

Joy   But what if I do?

Paul   Keep going. Smile and make sure they can hear you at the back. I was sick three times AND I had a seizure before my first show.

Anna   How many were in the audience again?

Morgan (*low*)   Over a thousand.

Paul   Over a thousand.

Ken   Wowee, I can't fathom . . .

Esther   Do you remember much about it?

Paul   Hardly. But when we came out for the curtain call there were all these bodies on their feet, clapping and screaming. You're faced with this wave of elation, and it swamps you . . . and the first one. The very first one, was the greatest feeling of my whole life.

Sheila   Like an organism?

Paul   Better, Sheila.

Joy *offers* **Paul** *a wipe.*

Joy   Have a wipe.

Paul   No thanks.

Joy   They're lemon-scented.

Morgan   If you fully commit to choir this week, that feeling Paul described is something we can all experience on Saturday.

Ken   Got it.

Morgan   I've also asked Freddie to sing at the gig, so he'll be rehearsing with us.

Anna   Exciting!

Paul   Does he know the arrangements?

Morgan   I've been teaching them during his lessons.

Joy   Is this Freddie allowed to sing on Saturday?

Morgan   Freddie's the young person we're helping and it's simply a way of showcasing his talent.

Paul   I hope introducing another tenor won't overpower the sound.

Morgan   Let me worry about the balance. You all enjoy the spotlight, show off! There are still a few tickets left so tell everyone you know, we want this place to be overflowing with ecstasy.

Sheila   Drug dealers?

Morgan   No.

Esther   I've got my tickets.

Joy   Let's hope the kids behave.

Esther   They do behave.

Joy   Jack took his willy out in Pizza Express.

Esther   That was years ago.

Anna   Ed and the kids can't make it unfortunately. Saturday's a busy day. Activities.

Morgan   Can't he bring the kids in the evening?

Anna   He's very busy. There are lots of activities. Every Saturday. And every evening. And on Sunday.

Sheila   I'm not bothering with other people.

Ken   Me neither.

Joy   I don't know any people.

Esther   If you made an effort to talk to the neighbours . . .

Joy   I talk to that Nigel.

Esther   You accused him of dumping garden waste in your green bin.

Joy   Well he did.

Esther   You didn't have to stick it on the WhatsApp.

Joy   He smeared fox shit on the lid.

Esther   You can't be certain, Joy.

Morgan   Everyone, Paul's boyfriend is coming.

Communal gasp of astonishment.

Sheila   What about his wife and four kids and the guinea pigs . . .?

Paul (*interrupts*)   They're splitting up.

Anna   Fantastic!

Esther   You deserve happiness.

Paul   Nobody talk to him please, he's painfully shy, so when you see him . . . ignore him.

Sheila   I hope he knows how lucky he is, having sex with you.

Ken   Imagine it, me performing with a West End star.

Paul   I wasn't exactly a star.

Anna *coughs.* **Joy** *takes out her wipes, offers* **Anna**.

Esther   'Course you were.

Paul   Remember, don't speak to him!

Joy   Have a wipe.

Anna   Oh, I'm fine.

Joy   They're very fresh.

Esther   She doesn't want one.

Their voices get louder.

Joy   Nobody's asking you.

Morgan   Please, you two . . .

Esther   She said no!

Freddie *tentatively enters. He's dressed in old-fashioned, badly-fitting jeans and top.*

Joy (*fierce*)   Don't you shitting well start on me, Esther!

Morgan   Freddie, Freddie . . . come in!

He gently waves at everyone.

Morgan   Welcome! This is the choir.

Paul   At last, the famous Freddie.

Freddie   Oh, I'm not anyone.

Anna   Not yet!

Morgan   Wait till you hear this boy's pipes! Come on, choir . . . er . . . introduce yourselves!

Esther   Esther.

Joy   Joy.

Esther *points at* **Joy**.

Esther   We're best friends.

Freddie   Hello.

Morgan   This is Sheila.

Sheila *gives him a hug. She doesn't let go.* **Morgan** *intervenes and gently prises* **Freddie** *away.*

Anna   Anna.

Esther   The concert was Anna's idea.

Ken   She's a charity person.

Sheila   For otters.

Freddie   It's my dream to go to music college, thank you . . . thank you so much.

Anna   I haven't done anything.

Morgan   She's too modest! Stop being so modest. It's weird.

Ken   I'm Ken.

Freddie   Hi there.

Ken   My wife left me.

Awkward pause.

Morgan   Come and sit down, Freddie.

Ken   She's not coming back. But I'm fine.

Morgan   Thanks, Ken.

Ken   Absolutely fine.

Paul   Paul.

Esther   He used to be in the West End.

Joy   Lionel Richie came to see him in his dressing room.

Paul   Not just me.

Joy   He touched him.

Paul   We shook hands.

Ken   He said you blew his mind.

Paul   It was a while ago.

Joy   Do you want a wipe?

Freddie   Er, no thanks.

Joy   You've come from outside. There's dirt outside.

Esther   Leave him alone, Joy.

Anna *moves towards the canvas, beckons* **Freddie**.

Anna   Take a look at this.

Freddie *joins her, his face contorts with discomfort.*

Freddie   What is it?

Esther   You.

Freddie   Er . . . okay, how did you know what I looked like?

Joy   I imagined you. In my brain.

Morgan   Joy's . . . artistic.

Joy   I speak French.

Esther   She's learning.

Morgan   It's going to be the backdrop to the gig. We felt we needed something that made a statement!

Awkward silence as they all stare at him.

Ken   Are you alright, Freddie?

Freddie   Yeah.

Morgan   Of course he's alright. Sorry if we're bombarding you . . . can we not bombard him, please?

Paul   Now your young man's here you can tell us your news, Morgan.

Morgan   Right . . . everyone gather round.

They form a circle round **Morgan**.

Morgan   As you all know we are doing this gig on Saturday to raise funds for this hugely talented singer to train so he can get started in the crazy business we call show. And . . . well . . . you're not going to believe it, but a production company approached me a few days ago, they're interested in Freddie's story and what we're doing to support him.

Esther   And?

Morgan   They want to shoot the gig, we're going to be on a television programme!

Silence.

Sheila   Oh God.

Esther   Oh my God.

Joy   Oh God.

Ken   You're not playing a sick joke on us, are you Morgan?

Morgan   It's not a joke . . . a camera crew and production team are coming here on Saturday.

Anna   Oh!

Sheila   Oh God.

Esther   Oh my God, oh my God, oh my God . . .

Sheila   Oh God.

Esther   God, God, God . . .

Sheila   Oh my God, oh my God!

Morgan   I know!

Esther   Oh God!

Freddie   Wow.

Joy   Fuck, fuck, fuck. Fuck!

Anna   Oh . . .

Sheila   God.

Esther   God.

Joy   Fuck.

Morgan   I realise it's a lot to take in . . .

Ken   Us on the telly?

Morgan   It's a segment for *The One Show*.

Joy   Jesus Christ, I love that programme. Fuck!

Morgan   It's a piece on the power of singing together. They're covering three choirs and we are one of them. They've asked for a photo of each of you and some background, which I'll send . . .

Anna   Such fantastic publicity.

Morgan   It means we can hopefully do more gigs, help more young people, possibly expand the choir. And it's all because of you, Freddie.

Freddie   This is a lot to take in, it's . . . much . . . bigger than I thought.

Paul   You're lucky, having all this effort put into you.

Freddie   I'll try not to let you down.

Paul   Don't you dare!

Morgan *moves to her laptop.*

Morgan   Of course he won't.

Esther   Look at him . . . he's clearly reliable.

Freddie   Usually.

Paul   How do you mean usually?

Freddie   I don't generally let people down.

Sheila   Yay!

Freddie   Apart from when . . . I dropped my sister's baby.

Awkward mumbles as they take this in.

Freddie   I was so scared of holding it, my hands were shaking and it sort of flopped out of my arms and . . . it didn't break anything . . . too bad. Just its index finger.

Morgan   Right.

Freddie   And its femur.

Anna   Was the baby okay?

Freddie   Oh, yeah.

Morgan   No harm done then.

Freddie   My mum says she'll never forgive me.

Esther   Give her time.

Freddie   My nephew's five now. Mum says I'm descended from the devil.

Morgan   We're all imperfect, complicated beings, aren't we?

Joy   Speak for yourself.

Anna   Everyone makes mistakes.

Sheila   I call them happy accidents. You dropping the baby and breaking its bones was a happy accident!

Uneasy pause.

Freddie   So there'll be cameras and everything on Saturday?

Morgan   Absolutely.

Freddie   Real cameras?

Morgan   We've got a lot to do, so let's carry on . . . Freddie, do join in.

Lizzo's 'Juice' starts to play.

The choir sing with their song sheets. After a verse or so, **Morgan** *pulls the music.*

Morgan   We're going to have to lose the sheets.

Ken   What?

Morgan   They make you look like amateurs.

Anna   We are amateurs.

Morgan   We don't have to shout about it.

Sheila   How will we know the words?

Morgan   You know them, Sheila.

Ken   I don't.

Esther   Me neither.

Morgan   You think you don't, but you do. Paul and I did loads of gigs when we were younger. It was nerve-racking but we never forgot our words because great song lyrics enter your bloodstream and become part of your muscle memory. Sheets down!

They put the pages down. **Morgan** *starts the music again.*

They all sway along but it's clear they don't know the words and they start to la and ooh and aah. **Morgan** *pulls the music.*

Morgan   Make sure you know the words to every song by the next rehearsal.

Joy   But there are fucking loads.

Morgan   We are going to be on BBC1! Alongside other choirs who have dance moves, children with missing teeth, matching T-shirts.

Esther   Can we have matching T-shirts?

Morgan   My choir would NEVER sink that low!

Ken   I'm worried I don't have time to practise.

Morgan   Ken, you haven't got a job.

Ken   Somehow . . . I'm always . . . stretched.

Morgan *takes the sheets from everyone, tears them up. They watch, aghast.*

Morgan   We are going to make this happen by leaning on each other and working together. It's going to be an intense few days but if you trust me, I promise, spectacular things are on their way.

Anna   Is there a dress code?

Morgan   Smart casual please. We want to look normal, so people can relate to us, but different enough so that they can also aspire to be us.

Ken   Are trousers and a shirt okay?

Morgan   Perfect. I appreciate you're all probably out of your comfort zones but that's how we improve performance.

Ken   So smart-casual trousers and a smart-casual shirt?

Morgan (*nods*)   Can I have sopranos and altos to go over the chorus for Coldplay?

Ken   Any trousers and any shirt?

Morgan   Yes!

The women go and sit by **Morgan**. *They go over a few lines and sing. Sounds of 'Fix You' under the following section.*

Ken *is learning his words on the other side.* **Paul** *finds* **Freddie**.

Paul   I hear you're going to be a star.

Freddie   I dunno.

Paul   Morgan thinks so. You'll need an agent.

Freddie   Really?

Paul   As soon as you get your agent, the best thing to do is pretend they've died. Imagine they fell down a man-hole or choked on a fish bone.

Freddie   Why?

Paul   Because they never call. They say they're going to call but . . .

Freddie   What?

Paul   You can send Krispy Kremes, orchids, stick a Russian Blue kitten in a box and courier it over. Tell them you've kidnapped their grandma. And nothing! (*A beat.*) Have you ever been tortured by a psychopath, Freddie?

Freddie Eh?

Paul You know, had pins stuck into your buttocks or wee poured on your head while you're tied to a chair.

Freddie *shakes his head.*

Paul Pity. It's fantastic preparation for the business. (*A beat.*) Anyway, it's a delight to have you.

Freddie I'd like to be like you. One day.

Paul Me?

Freddie They said you're big.

Paul I was poised, ready to launch, but I'd go up for auditions and come second and then my career went up my nose . . . I do voice work now. Mainly local radio. If you hear an advert for a bargain basement car showroom with two stars on Trustpilot, that'll be me.

Freddie Incredible.

Paul I make my money. I just replaced my sash windows. Hardwood. Triple glazing.

Freddie And you and Morgan used to sing together?

Paul Centuries ago. You'll find that the people who run the business are interested in right now, in what's fresh and young. They believe that a new take will help us to understand old things.

Freddie That's deep.

Paul I talk facts not philosophy. What matters is, all that really matters is . . . that I've got a sweet boyfriend who adores me. Do you want to see a picture?

Paul *takes out his phone. The women come back to the group.* **Morgan** *is on the laptop.*

Ken   I reckon this news about the telly warrants a new outfit. I'd like to be fresh, you know, clean.

Esther   Aren't you normally clean?

Ken   Depends if there's soap left. Sometimes the bar dissolves in my hand.

Sheila   Same!

Ken   Anyway, this is an opportunity for me to feel brand new. Shirt, trousers, belt, shoes, socks. And a vest and pants.

Joy   Do they still do Y fronts?

Freddie   Y fronts?

Joy   You don't hear people mention them any more.

Anna   No, you really don't.

Joy   Quel dommage.

Sheila   They do do them. (*A beat.*) The men's section is my favourite. Sometimes I open packets of fancy socks and put my hand in and touch them. I know it's illegal, but I feel them anyway!

Ken   Wish I had your courage, Sheila.

Sheila   Share mine, Ken. You need some in this life. Otherwise you get trampled on.

Ken   I'm not sure how to go about buying everything. My wife . . . used to . . . er . . .

Morgan   You find a shop and pick stuff and buy it.

Ken   Which shop?

Esther   One that sells men's clothes.

Ken   What do I choose?

Anna   Whatever you like.

Ken   But how do I know what I like?

Morgan   You just do.

Ken   I don't. I really don't.

Anna   Get everything online.

Ken   I'm no good at that.

Esther   We'll sort something out.

Morgan   Quiet please! First two verses and chorus.

Mash up between 'Seven Nation Army' and Eurythmics' 'Sweet Dreams' plays. **Morgan** *conducts as the choir sing along.* **Freddie** *is phenomenal.*

When the music stops, **Paul** *pointedly gathers his stuff – coat, bag, etc. And noisily moves his chair. He starts to walk out.*

Morgan   Paul, what are you doing?

Paul   You clearly don't . . . need me any more.

Esther   Of course we do!

Sheila   Nobody can do what you do.

Joy   Lionel Richie knows.

Freddie   Was I singing too loud?

Paul   No. I mean, you were a bit.

Ken   As a fellow tenor, I don't feel whole without you, Paul.

Anna   Come back! Please, Paul . . .

Esther   We can't sing without you.

Paul   You can.

Joy   Morgan, make him stay!

Morgan (*to* **Paul**)   You are part of this choir!

Paul   I fear I've become the bottom end of a straggly, overgrown fringe . . .

Morgan   None of this works without you, Paul.

Paul   Are you sure?

Morgan   Yes.

Paul (*a beat*)   Well . . . perhaps I'll stay for a bit.

He loudly puts his stuff down and returns to the group. **Anna** *gets a message on her phone.*

Freddie   How many cameras do you think there'll be on Saturday?

Morgan   I don't know.

Freddie   More than one though?

Morgan   Forget about the cameras.

Esther   Joy, we don't sing the first line of the second verse and you sang the first line of the second verse.

Joy   I didn't.

Esther   I heard you.

Joy   Might be time to get the wax removed from your ears again.

Esther   And we've got the melody, not the harmony. You're sounding a bit soprano.

Joy   I am not.

Anna *gets up, starts moving around with her phone.*

Morgan   Esther, it's not for you to judge what Joy's . . .

Esther (*interrupts*)   It's *The One Show*! It has to be right.

Joy *walks off and positions herself on the other side of the room.*

Morgan   I need the altos together.

Joy   She's putting me off.

Anna *continues to wander around.*

Morgan   We won't get the right sound for the gig.

Joy   I'll sit here for the rehearsal then.

Freddie *turns to* **Anna**.

Freddie   Are you okay?

Anna   I'm looking for a signal.

Morgan   You don't need a signal at the moment.

Esther *points to the back chair.*

Esther   You normally get one there, don't you?

Anna   Not tonight.

Freddie   She doesn't look okay.

Morgan   Anna, can you stop moving . . .

Anna   No, I can't . . . I really can't . . .

Sheila *starts playing with the roller skates.*

Ken   It's been raining. Water droplets absorb a certain radio frequency and partially block the access to the router.

Freddie   How do you know that?

Morgan   Anna!

Ken   Often when I'm listening to the radio or watching my dinner rotate in the microwave, a thought or a question occurs to me and I'll look it up on the internet. Sometimes even write down the answer in my notebook.

He takes his notebook out, shows **Freddie**.

Ken   Before I got made redundant, I was in charge of installing sprinkler systems in motorway service stations. I can show you some diagrams if you like.

He flicks through the notebook. **Sheila** *wheels herself around on one skate.*

Freddie (*to* **Morgan**)   Will the cameras be on me?

Morgan   Yeah!

Paul   A performer has to fall in lust with the camera, isn't that right, Morgan?

Anna *is still moving.* **Sheila** *starts to whizz herself around the space.*

Ken   We bring our best selves to choir, Freddie. And choir seems to bring out the best in us. We have our ups and downs, but generally you'll find we're a happy bunch.

Sheila *knocks into* **Morgan***, who stumbles.*

Morgan (*shouts*)   Will you please all just fucking well do what I say?

They all stare at her, bemused.

Morgan   I mean . . . can we focus on the music?

Joy   Yeah.

Esther   Definitely.

Anna   Sure.

Sheila   Not a problem.

Paul   It's only about the music.

Ken   Don't you worry, Morgan, everything's going to be marvellous.

Morgan   Of course . . . it's all . . . going to be marvellous.

Scene change as they all sing 'Sweet Dreams'.

Scene Two – Wednesday

Sheila, **Ken**, **Anna** *and* **Freddie** *are sitting together.* **Ken** *is apprehensively looking over a song sheet.*

Sheila   Are you ready?

Ken   Give me a minute.

Anna   Ken . . .

Ken   Please . . .

Anna   Be confident!

She takes the sheet away.

Ken   There are so many words, they're jumbling up in my mouth.

Freddie   You almost did it . . .

Ken   Only because you lot helped. Morgan won't allow that on the night. Needing help isn't professional.

Sheila   Go over it a few times now and you'll get there for Saturday.

Ken   I don't want to disappoint her.

Anna   Sheila's right, let's continue.

Freddie   I'll count you in . . .

Sheila   Nice deep breath, Ken.

They all stand and face each other.

Freddie   One, two, three.

Anna *plays music on her phone.*

Ken *braces himself and starts singing the first verse of Beyoncé's 'Crazy in Love'. As he sings, the others pointedly mime a few key words, e.g. eyes/touch/kiss to help him remember.*

They all join in with the chorus and continue to mime the key actions.

Morgan *enters, slightly agitated.*

They all finish the song and cheer. **Anna** *stops the music.*

Morgan   How come you're so early?

Sheila   We're practising for the television people.

Morgan   I'm impressed. I'd usually be here by now, but my bike's gone awol.

Anna   Oh no.

Morgan *takes off her coat, starts setting up her music equipment.*

Anna   What happened?

Morgan   It was outside Morrisons, thought I'd locked it but . . . oh, it doesn't matter. It's a piece of junk. Then I had to wait ages for the bus . . . the 261 is like an elusive lover.

Ken   I never touch the 261. It's a heinous route.

Morgan   So how do you get here?

Ken   I take the 48, then the 391 and the 7 or the 83.

Morgan   But that means you do zig-zags through town, must take hours.

Morgan*'s phone beeps. She checks it.*

Ken   Oh, it does. But you get to see the drunks relieving themselves at the back of the old church and those huge 4 by 4s driving into the shopping centre, and up the hill there's a splendid view of the sheep sculptures on the new estate.

Morgan   Who wants to see that?

She replies to the message.

Ken   They're lives being lived, Morgan. All of us with our wins and losses and we're together on this planet, breathing the same air. It's a . . . a comfort.

Anna   You should write a memoir, Ken. You're so . . . alive.

Morgan*'s phone beeps again. She is getting increasingly stressed.*

Sheila   You might get invited to the Hay Festival. What do you reckon, Morgan?

Morgan *replies to the message.*

Morgan   Possibly.

Freddie   And, he's practically word perfect.

Morgan Well done!

Ken I'm not.

Anna When he sings the verse it's like listening to Beyoncé's identical twin.

Freddie Everyone here's really nice.

Morgan *gets another message.*

Morgan Everyone's nice when you first meet them. When you get to know someone, that's when the darkness appears.

Sheila I'm horrible.

Morgan No, you're not . . .

Sheila But I am slowly improving.

Morgan I was joking, Sheila.

Esther *and* **Joy** *come in, they're holding hands.*

Esther Hello.

Joy Hello.

Phone goes again. **Morgan** *reads the message.*

Esther We've decided to start afresh. Because we're best friends.

Joy Neighbours actually.

Esther Neighbours who are best friends. And when we're on television we're going to look happy, aren't we?

Joy I'm always happy.

Morgan *replies to the message, tries to mask her stress.*

Esther Not always, Joy.

Joy I'm always happy inside, Esther. You can't see my insides.

Morgan   Okay, there've been a few emails flying around with the production company. I'm going to make some minor, well tiny but significant . . . adjustments to the show . . .

She checks her computer. **Esther** *hands* **Ken** *a large bag.*

Esther   Got you a selection of Dave's bits and pieces.

Ken   I'm a lucky, lucky man.

Esther   Try a few bits on and see how you go.

Joy *picks up a paint brush, starts painting on the canvas.*

Sheila *and* **Ken** *rummage through the bag.* **Paul** *saunters in wearing a trendy and flamboyant jacket.*

Ken *finds some clothes and starts taking his own clothes off.*

Anna (*to* **Paul**)   Gorgeous!

Paul   James watched the last episode of *Strictly* with his wife, so I threw a Le Creuset at him. We broke up.

Esther   That's awful.

Paul   Not really . . . because while he was on the trolley in A and E, we made up. (*Indicates jacket.*) He bought me this old thing from McQueen. And we had Five Guys in bed.

Sheila   Yum.

Paul   And he sent me a slice of luxury cheese made from donkey milk. And he's taking me to a rooftop restaurant the night before the gig. I've checked the menu and I'm having soufflé de fromage, longe de veau followed by tarte de citron avec crème anglaise!

The others notice that **Ken** *is almost naked, down to his pants.*

Morgan (*shocked*)   Ken, what are you doing?

Ken   Esther told me to get changed.

Esther   Not here!

Paul   Who cares? I don't.

Paul *grabs him and sings 'I Feel Pretty' as they dance across the space together.* **Paul** *twirls* **Ken** *and he spins off on his own and* **Esther** *immediately tries to cover him up.*

Ken   Sorry, I forget about other people.

Ken *takes the clothes and puts them on.*

Ken   I'm only around human bodies when I come here.

Morgan   It's okay.

Sheila   I never remember to lock public toilets.

Ken *shows off his clothes. They are ill-fitting and badly mismatched. He tries to be enthusiastic.*

Ken   Smart casual enough?

Anna   You don't look very comfortable.

Ken   I'll get used to it.

Anna *helps* **Ken** *find some better clothes.*

Morgan   So, the television people have suggested we do a duet.

Joy *and* **Anna** *start to sing Elton John's 'Don't Go Breaking My Heart'.*

Esther *walks around to look at the canvas.*

Morgan   No, it's the wrong tone . . .

Esther   What is that?

Joy   What?

Esther   On his head, that . . .

Joy   Isn't it obvious?

The others gather round, mystified.

Joy   It's a Frida Kahlo headdress.

Esther   Why?

Joy   Symbolises his artistic expression. Plus it makes him interesting. No offence, Freddie, but you're not interesting.

Esther   Looks . . . odd.

Joy   Morgan asked *me* to do this painting.

Esther (*to* **Morgan**)   You said I could help.

Morgan   Well . . .

Joy   Assist. She said you could be my assistant. Because *you* didn't get a B in your Art GCSE, did you, Esther?

Esther   I didn't do Art GCSE.

Joy   Exactement!

Esther   It's making me feel . . . uncomfortable.

Joy   Do you want a wipe?

Esther   No thanks.

Freddie   I don't mind a headdress.

Morgan   Let's leave it.

Esther   Okay.

Ken   How about . . . (*Sings.*) My love, there's only you in my life. The only thing that's right . . .

Morgan   Too obvious. There's actually an arrangement I've been wanting to share but it's . . . difficult . . .

Paul   What's the song?

Morgan   You're all I need to get by. Marvin Gaye and . . .

Esther   Tammi!

Paul   We used to do that, years ago.

Anna (*to* **Freddie**)   Morgan and Paul had a band.

Freddie   An actual band?

Paul   We did weddings.

Morgan   Not at the beginning. We got together at college. I wrote the songs. Paul was the frontman. We had things to say about homelessness, war, poverty.

Joy   Sounds fun.

Morgan   Remember . . . (*sings in a punk fashion*) I am broken in my heart, ravaged in my soul, dead in my bones, I am dead . . . dead . . .

Paul   Oh yes.

Morgan   They were vibrant songs. Radical songs that . . . were about . . . humanity!

Paul   People didn't really go for them though.

Morgan   We had a following!

Paul   Until we started doing cover versions at weddings. Not nice weddings. Ones where the bride and groom didn't like each other and noses got broken.

Anna   They almost got signed by a record company.

Morgan   I had spiky blue hair and my skin was flawless. We were going to change the world.

Freddie   So what happened?

Morgan   The big break didn't materialise and we went our separate ways, I got my job at the FE college . . . and the years passed and recently I realised how much I missed making music. So I started thinking about setting up a choir, got in touch with Paul and put a few posters up . . .

Ken   There was one in the GP surgery.

Esther   And in Morrisons.

Sheila   And in the police station.

Morgan   And here we are.

Joy   Who came up with the shit name?

Freddie   What is the name?

Ken   The Morgan Jackson People's Choir.

Paul (*indicates* **Morgan**)   She wanted something snappy that rolled off the tongue.

Morgan   I'm not changing it.

Sheila *takes out a Greggs carrier bag.*

Sheila   Vegan sausage roll, anyone?

They each gravitate towards **Sheila** *and take a sausage roll.*

Esther   These look good.

Anna   So good, Sheila.

Sheila   Really?

Anna   Mmmm . . .

Sheila   I made them in front of *Bake Off.*

Freddie *looks at the carrier bag.*

Freddie   But that bag . . .

Sheila   Yes.

Freddie   It's a Greggs bag.

Sheila   I used that because it was in the carrier bag drawer, it was the one at the top.

Awkward silence.

Ken   Perhaps the carrier bag is a red herring.

Freddie   They look like the ones from the shop . . .

Sheila (*interrupts*)   They're from my kitchen!

Freddie   I don't reckon so.

Morgan   Let's say they are.

Anna   They are because they are.

Sheila   Doesn't sound like he believes me.

Morgan   He does, don't you Freddie?

Freddie   Er . . . okay.

Sheila   I won't make them again.

Esther   Please make them again.

Ken   These are nectar from the Gods.

Sheila   Oh, alright then.

Anna   Thank you, Sheila. (*To* **Freddie**.) She adores baking, you see.

Sheila   I hate it. But they love them so much, what can I do?

Morgan   So, 'You're All I Need'!

Paul   I'm not convinced.

Esther   Whitney, Morgan, just this once.

Morgan   Never!

Freddie   Why not Whitney?

Morgan   Too obvious. Too . . . I feel there are certain artists that should remain untouched. Like 'Over the Rainbow'. Nobody else should sing that song.

The choir pointedly start singing a rendition of 'Over the Rainbow'. It's joyful and uplifting. **Morgan** *smiles but signals to them to stop.*

Morgan   This isn't karaoke. We're using our voices as a collective to transport our audience.

Paul   I'm not sure my voice can cope with 'You're All I Need' now.

Morgan   Doesn't matter.

Paul   Morgan, it didn't fly back then, the top notes were always a stretch.

Morgan   That's why I want Freddie to do it.

Silence.

Freddie   Me?

Morgan   Yes.

Freddie   But . . . I don't know it.

Morgan   As a singer, you have to be nimble, get to know a song fast, make it your new best friend.

She turns to the others and presses a button on her phone.

Morgan   I'm sending the other parts now, I realise it's a mammoth task but if we get this right, we're going to achieve something that none of us have ever achieved.

Joy   You must be flushing something down the toilet to make room for Marvin Gaye . . .

Morgan   Primal Scream.

Anna   But that's Paul's song.

Morgan   I have to take into consideration the flow and cadence of the whole night.

Esther   His boyfriend's coming.

Morgan   Paul, I should have said, there's been a lot to do . . . sorry.

Awkward silence.

Ken (*to* **Paul**)   You okay?

Paul   James will be here anyway.

Sheila   I think his feelings are hurt but he's not saying.

Paul   My feelings are not anything.

Morgan   Paul's an old boot. Robust enough to climb Everest.

Freddie   I don't mind not doing it.

Esther   Not your fault, sweetheart. I'm just . . . Morgan, you've always, since day one, given everyone a chance to shine.

Morgan   You are all, always shining. This is a performance. A performance is different. Paul gets it.

Paul   Of course I do.

Morgan *glances at her phone.*

Morgan   I have to reply to this. Begin learning your sections off the Dropbox. Freddie, Anna will be doing the duet with you.

Freddie   I haven't got a smartphone.

Morgan   What?

Esther   Why not?

Freddie   Can't afford one.

Anna   You can share mine.

Morgan *retreats to the side. The others all look at* **Paul**.

Paul   Nobody speak.

Sheila   Paul looks sad . . .

Paul   Nobody!

They go to sit in their sections and using their phones/headphones, they start learning the words. As they do this, they continue to be in the space – going over words, etc.

Esther *paints on the canvas.*

Lines they are singing can cut across the dialogue.

Ken   I'll get the drinks. Freddie, what's your poison?

Freddie   Lemonade.

Ken   And?

Freddie   A glass.

Ken *exits.* **Anna** *sits with* **Freddie**. *They do a section from 'You're All I Need'.*

Freddie   I've upset them.

Anna   No.

Freddie   It's what I do.

Anna   People get upset, we all get upset and then . . . twenty-four hours later, we're okay.

He takes some knitting from a bag, starts to knit. **Anna** *watches.*

Anna   What's that?

Freddie   A balaclava.

Anna   Oh . . .

Freddie   Do you want one?

Anna   No.

Freddie   I can't make anything else. Arguments aren't . . . I don't like them. This helps.

His knitting gets more frenetic and then he stops.

Anna   My son's a worrier. He's wonderful. But quite . . . he feels everything . . . like a wound, you know? They say alpha fathers have beta sons. Have you heard that?

He shakes his head.

Anna   So . . . you love singing?

Freddie   It's the only thing I can do.

Anna   Well you are extremely good at something and that's enough.

Freddie   So are you.

Ken *brings drinks in, hands them out.*

Anna   I'm just very grateful.

Freddie   For?

Anna   Everything. (*Half joking.*) My husband sometimes wishes I was less average but, this is me.

Esther *goes to the canvas, picks up a paintbrush.*

Freddie   Sheila is . . . weird.

Anna   You're making a balaclava.

Freddie   But she's not telling the truth.

Anna   What's the truth?

Freddie   You know what I mean.

Anna   Freddie, you come to choir and watch and listen and your heart can just . . . beat. You can love people here and they don't even know, but they . . . feel something from you. And you feel something back . . .

Anna's *phone vibrates. She hurriedly answers it.*

Anna   Hello . . . hello sweetheart . . . okay . . . yeah . . . he's busy probably . . . I can read it if you like . . . give me a few minutes . . . go to the toilet and call me back. Love you.

She comes off the phone.

Anna   Have you got a partner?

Freddie *shakes his head.*

Anna   Make sure you wait. For a long time. The longest. And if the singing doesn't work out straight away, I mean it will eventually, how about you get a nice job in Pizza Express? Work your way up to assistant manager. Be part of a clockwork machine serving customers. Fill their stomachs and get them drunk. Make them happy. And at the end of your shift go out dancing with your team and then go home and sleep. And the next morning you get up and do it all over again. It's simple . . . and it's all you do. It starts and it ends, nothing else. I would love that. I'd really love it.

Freddie   People . . . are too much for me.

Anna   Yeah. (*A beat.*) Can I show you something?

Then takes out a ring box, gives it to **Freddie**. *He takes it out.*

Anna   It's an eternity ring.

Freddie   I've never heard of that.

Anna   Represents neverending love. Do you want it?

Freddie   What?

Anna   It's worth thousands. You could sell it. Or save it for your special person.

Freddie   No, thank you.

Anna   Please, have it . . .

Freddie *puts the box down.*

Morgan *goes to the laptop and 'You're All I Need' music starts to play.*

Morgan   Once through together please.

They all sing 'You're All I Need', **Morgan** *conducts with passion but it's really bad.*

Paul   That was a disaster movie where the whole cast perishes.

Joy *heads to the canvas.*

Esther   Sounded like a farm.

Morgan   We'll get there. We will . . .

Joy *regards the canvas. Her face fills with dismay.*

Joy   Bars . . . across his face?

Esther   The idea is that singing lets him out of the prison of society. It . . . releases him.

Joy   You've been listening to a podcast again!

Morgan Joy . . .

Joy She's made it literal, obvious! I was trying to create something unique and beautiful.

Esther By putting dandelions on his head?

Joy It's figurative! Fucking hell . . .

Morgan *intervenes.*

Morgan Calm down. The producers are interested in us, in our individual stories and I've told them that you've been best friends since primary school.

Joy She never talked to me at primary school.

Esther We were in different schools!

Morgan The point is you've known each other a long time.

Joy Everyone stayed away from me back then.

Esther Because you used to say bizarre things.

Joy I was imaginative. Mrs Baker said I might become an artist.

Esther You told everyone you had green skin. Why would you do that?

Morgan Stop it, both of you! The television people are coming to interview you. Millions are going to be watching and that audience has to believe in you, to even . . . want to be you for a few minutes. They need to hear that you started your periods on the same day and take turns basting the turkey at Christmas and that you delivered Esther's first-born in a Topshop changing room. So please for the sake of a young man's future, start looking like you'd take a bullet for each other!

Joy *and* **Esther** *both smile, reluctantly.*

Paul They're doing interviews?

Morgan On the morning of the show.

Sheila   Ken could share one of his poems.

Morgan   They don't do poetry on *The One Show*.

Esther   That Carol Ann Duffy was on the other week!

Sheila   She can't touch Ken, wait till you hear one of his.

Joy   Go on.

Ken   My work's quite . . . personal.

Anna   It's only us.

Paul   Speak, man!

Ken *braces himself.*

Ken   I'm sad, sad, sad I tell ya. I feel so bad it's making me mad. I look in the mirror and all I see is my dad. It's too bad I tell ya, too bad.

Silence.

Sheila   Ask *The One Show*, won't you Morgan, if they can fit him in.

Morgan   I will. Everyone must practise 'You're All I Need' but for now . . . let's try Amy.

Anna *starts moving around, trying to get a signal again.*

Morgan   This is your solo, Anna.

Anna   My son's going to call. He wants me to read him his story.

Morgan   Get Ed to do it.

Anna   Ed's busy.

Morgan   You're needed here!

Anna*'s phone rings.*

Anna   Hi darling, I've got it on my phone . . . yes. (*She reads from 'The Tiger Who Came to Tea' by Judith Kerr.*)

Anna *moves to the side.*

Anna   Now you read . . .

Fed up, **Morgan** *addresses the others.*

Morgan   Okay, positions for the show!

She takes each person and places them on the small platform at the back. She positions **Ken** *to the far left.*

Morgan   That's it. That's us.

There'll be an extra rehearsal on Friday evening.

Ken   Another one?

Morgan   I am not being turned into a meme!

Under pressure, **Morgan** *retreats to her laptop.*

Morgan   They've asked me to finalise the running order. If you head into the bar, I'll call you and we'll go over Amy.

The singers disperse. **Anna** *leaves but remains on her phone.*

Paul *lingers, waits still everyone has left.*

Paul (*shouts*)   'You're All I Fucking Need'!

Morgan   It was one of their suggestions.

Paul   You could have countered with a suggestion of your own.

Morgan   The producers want to showcase Freddie.

Paul   Oh yes, your great young hope.

Morgan   There's a nasty tinge in your voice and there's no need for a nasty tinge.

Paul   You really think he's special.

Morgan   Yes.

Paul *makes a face.*

Morgan   You said you were alright.

Paul   I'm not going to say anything in front of them, am I?

Morgan   Them? Let's not patronise anyone, Paul, they are us and we are them.

Paul   You choosing that song is nostalgic bullshit!

Morgan   If you don't like my choices, you're free to go!

Paul   You asked me to be part of this . . . charade.

Morgan   Leave then! Go on, get lost!

Paul   What's wrong with you?

Morgan   I'm . . . tired.

Paul   Everyone over forty's tired, Morgan.

Morgan   I am tired of looking after everyone, of managing seven different personalities. Each one needs something different. And I can't always . . . I haven't always got it.

Paul   You love bossing everyone. Controlling, organising, perfecting . . .

Morgan   . . . massaging egos! And some of those egos are big, Paul, quite enormous! I'm sorry about the duet, okay, but a lot of this is . . . it's out of my hands.

Paul   Forget it.

Silence.

Morgan   I'll ask if we can do Primal Scream as the encore.

Paul *shrugs.*

Morgan   It's the least you deserve.

Paul   Nobody deserves anything. You roll the dice and that's that.

Morgan   I'm sorry. It's . . . the pressure . . . Saturday means a lot, we have to pull this off. We have to.

Paul   First concert, first cut. It's the deepest.

Morgan   I sent the information to the producers about everyone. And the photos.

Paul   Did you use my Spotlight picture?

Morgan   I did.

Paul   2005 or 2008?

Morgan   Eight.

Paul   Thank God. (*A beat.*) My agent said when she squinted, I looked like George Clooney.

Morgan   Totally. (*A beat.*) You were so beautiful.

Paul   That was then . . .

He goes to leave.

Morgan   They've asked me to lose Ken.

Paul *stops.*

Paul   What?

Morgan   The producers, they don't want him to sing in the choir.

Paul   Why?

Morgan   They've said he . . . they've said he looks like a serial killer.

Silence.

Paul   Which one?

Morgan   I didn't ask, did I?

Paul   So tell them to fuck off.

Morgan   Obviously.

Paul   Good.

Morgan   I mean . . . I'm going to . . . once I find the right moment.

Paul   What?

Morgan   I've got a lot on, managing all of this, teaching at the college during the day.

Paul   They don't even care what we sound like, do they?

Morgan   Of course they care.

Paul   Fuck this, fucking shit business. I had a lucky escape.

Morgan   You still do your voiceovers.

Paul   I turn up so I can put food on the table. That's all. I give my outsides, not my insides. And this is why, this is the exact reason why.

Silence.

Paul   He's learnt all the words. Every single ooh and ah.

Morgan   I've only just found out. They keep making demands.

Paul   Until there's nothing left of you. Of your thing. Of who you are. I get it. We know it. (*A beat.*) Make sure you tell them.

Morgan   I will.

Paul   We'll still do the gig for Freddie, but without . . . *The One Show* shit. There's no choice here, you know that.

Morgan   Yes.

Paul   Seriously, Morgan. Seriously! You cancel this whole television thing, right?

Morgan   Absolutely.

Paul (*a beat*) How did the production company know about the gig in the first place?

Morgan   Social media. They find out everything. You know what it's like.

Paul   Yeah.

Paul *heads out.* **Morgan** *is left on her own.*

The choir come back on stage and sing Amy Winehouse's 'Back to Black' over the scene change. **Anna**'s *solo.*

Sheila *picks up the ring box which* **Anna** *has left. She opens it.*

Interval.

Scene Three – Friday

The choir (except **Paul***) are in their performance positions and are singing George Michael's 'Freedom'.* **Freddie** *is doing lead vocals and* **Morgan** *is conducting.*

Sheila *is wearing a prominent pair of mittens.*

Paul *enters and observes. He gets on the stage and joins in. The song comes to an end.*

Morgan   Nice.

Paul *puts his arm around* **Ken** *and points at him.*

Paul   This guy's the real backbone of the tenors.

Ken   Me?

Paul *and* **Ken** *sing the song together.*

Paul   Special, isn't he Morg?

Morgan *checks her laptop.*

Paul   Morgan?

Morgan   Oh . . . yes.

Morgan *regards* **Freddie** *and sings a line.*

Freddie *repeats the line.*

Morgan   Lower at the end.

Morgan   Better. Well done everybody.

The choir relax for a moment. **Morgan** *turns to* **Paul** *as she checks her laptop.*

Morgan   Shouldn't you be eating soufflé and canoodling in a rooftop restaurant?

Paul   I can do that anytime.

Morgan   He hasn't called?

Paul   No.

Morgan   Can you call him?

Paul   No.

Morgan   Sorry he's so shit.

Paul   James will be here for the show.

Morgan   Right.

Paul (*a beat*)   Why did you say 'Right' like that?

Morgan   What?

Paul   You said 'Right'. Not 'Right'. Not 'Right' like you were agreeing. You said 'Right' as if . . . he's not coming . . .

Morgan   Maybe because he's always letting you down . . .

Paul   Not always . . .

Morgan   I don't want you getting lost in someone's fantasy.

Paul   Our relationship is real. James is real. He left a sock in my bedroom.

Morgan   A single sock?

Paul   I'll bring it in.

Morgan *turns to the choir, takes a deep breath. She observes them closely.*

Morgan   Sheila, why the hell are you wearing mittens?

Sheila My extremities freeze up . . . you see my kidneys get overloaded and the heat leaves my body. Started when I was little and my dad used to forget my name.

Anna What did he call you?

Sheila Geoff.

Esther Okay.

Sheila After our next-door neighbour. He was round our house a lot . . . I think my dad liked him better than us.

Anna That's sad.

Sheila Not really, Geoff died in a car crash.

Morgan Take them off please.

Ken What if she catches a cold?

Morgan Mittens scream community choir.

Anna We are a community choir.

Morgan No, we are a choir *for* the community. There's a difference. Off!

Sheila *takes them off. Starts fussing with her hands.* **Morgan** *gets an alert on her phone.*

Morgan We just sold out!

Esther Oh God.

Joy Fuck.

Paul Shit.

Morgan This is . . . actually happening.

Joy *and* **Esther** *walk to the picture which is covered with a sheet.*

Joy The backdrop . . . c'est fini.

They all move towards it. **Joy** *and* **Esther** *stand by the canvas with pride.*

Esther   We decided to compromise.

Joy   Because what's important is we help this young person.

Esther   And because we're best friends.

Joy *removes the sheet. The choir recoil, they are all visibly shocked.*

Freddie   Is that what I look like?

Joy   This isn't you any more. It's its own being.

Anna   Is it human?

Esther/Joy   Yes/No.

Sheila *continues to play with her hands.*

Esther   Maybe we should colour the face in a bit more, make it clearer.

Joy   That'd ruin the contrast between the foreground and the distant horizon.

Esther   They're confused.

Morgan   It's completely fine.

Joy   Thank you!

Morgan *gets another message. Covers her concern.*

Morgan   Joy, can I borrow you to check the alto line with Freddie and Paul?

Joy *moves to the other side where* **Morgan** *conducts as* **Joy** *and the two men do the part from 'Freedom'.*

Meanwhile, **Esther** *surreptitiously takes a paintbrush and makes some strokes on the canvas. She signals to* **Anna**.

Esther   Now, everybody will understand!

Ken *and* **Sheila** *are at the back.* **Ken** *notes that* **Sheila** *is fiddling with her hands.*

Ken   Itchy hands, Sheila?

Sheila   Slightly.

Ken   I hope it's not hives.

Sheila   What's that?

Ken   Little bumps on your skin that show up when you're not quite right inside.

Sheila   I'll probably get them then.

Ken   I get them seasonally. Seasonal hives. GP gives me an injection, so I can cope.

Sheila   I'm glad you've found a way to cope.

They share a shy smile.

Morgan   Back in your sections, please!

Paul *catches sight of a ring on* **Sheila***'s finger.*

Paul   Those are some rocks, Sheila.

They all look at the ring.

Sheila   Oh, this . . . was my grandmother's.

Ken   Exquisite.

Sheila   She gave it to me on her deathbed. It had been given to her by her grandmother on her deathbed. And she said the same words to me that her grandmother had said to her.

The choir eye her expectantly.

Sheila   She said . . . er . . . she said . . . 'Where you lead, I will follow. Anywhere that you tell me to. If you need, you need me to be with you. I will follow where you lead.'

Silence.

Anna   How . . . beautiful.

Sheila   And then she told me never to take it off. But I forgot she'd said that and I found it the other day . . . next to the Cheerios.

Morgan   That's a lovely story, Sheila.

Esther   Very moving.

Morgan   So, I've had a thought about the start of the show . . .

Freddie   Wait . . .

Morgan   Time to sing, Freddie.

Freddie   That's not her ring!

They all stop.

Freddie   It's Anna's, she showed me the other day.

Anna   I showed you a ring, yes.

Freddie   She must have found it and picked it up.

Sheila *gasps, upset.*

Morgan   If Sheila says it's her ring . . .

Sheila   I said it was my grandmother's.

Esther   That's right, you did.

Sheila   Her name was Pam . . .

Paul   She sounds cute.

Sheila   She was. Dear Pam . . . Pamela . . . Anderson.

Freddie   The words she said on her deathbed are from a song.

Sheila   My Pamela Anderson was poetic.

Freddie   It's not true!

Sheila   I thought people here trusted me.

Morgan   Of course we do.

Sheila   I don't understand what's going on.

Freddie   You're lying.

Ken   The fact is, Freddie, everyone in choir's got different personalities. I'm rather slow off the mark.

Anna   I'm forever making lists.

Joy   I'm too fucking laid back.

Freddie   Admit it!

Sheila   He doesn't believe me.

Morgan   It doesn't matter what anyone thinks.

Sheila *is getting upset.*

Sheila   It does. Because my mum and dad didn't believe me either. Nobody did. I told the truth but none of them listened and that's why they banished me from Hounslow.

Freddie   You steal stuff!

Sheila   I make unwanted things feel wanted.

Silence.

Sheila   Because no matter what people think, they have a right to be in the world.

Morgan   It's okay, Sheila.

Sheila *holds out the ring, gives it to* **Anna**.

Sheila   I won't do it any more.

Anna *shakes her head.*

Anna   You have it. It's yours.

Freddie   She obviously needs help.

Morgan   Sheila's one of those people who's been through things. We don't need to know what they are. When we are in this room, we do not judge anybody who walks through that door.

Freddie   I'm being honest!

Morgan   You dropped a baby, Freddie!

Freddie   Yeah . . .

Morgan   That was a huge mistake. And you know what, you're going to make more. Bigger ones. Terrible ones that will plague you for years and years. You will hurt people and they will hurt you and sometimes you will want to murder and other times you will want to die and that's just . . . that's the way it is, Freddie. So let's sing. We're here to sing. That's something we can do and at least be better than we are . . . out there. Plus, we're doing it for you. We don't have to do it for you. But we are doing it for you, even though you dropped a baby! Okay?

Freddie *nods awkwardly.*

Morgan   Sheila . . . are you alright to continue?

Sheila *nods.*

Morgan   Let's go through Edge please.

The choir move into their sections. **Morgan** *plays music. Conducts the different sections as they do their parts.*

They carry on. After a few bars, **Morgan** *cuts the music.*

Morgan   What's this song about? Anyone?

Silence.

Freddie   Is it about a white winged dove?

Morgan   No.

Anna   Coming of age?

Morgan *shakes her head.*

Esther   Falling in love for the first time!

Morgan   This masterpiece explores spiritual release.

Ken   Right.

Morgan   Freedom. Death. Sex.

Joy   I knew that already.

Morgan   To make this work, you have to connect with the raw power inside you. Deep, raw power.

Unsure murmurs of agreement.

Morgan *plays the music and they sing 'Edge of Seventeen' once more.*

Halfway through, **Joy** *wanders towards the picture and picks up the paint palette, but when she looks at the painting she makes a wailing animalistic sound while falling to her knees.*

Morgan *cuts the music.*

Morgan   Joy?

Joy *eyes* **Esther.**

Joy   What have you done?

Esther   A few finishing touches. You can hardly see them . . .

But before she can finish, **Joy** *attacks the picture and tears it apart.*

Esther *tries to stop her but cannot. Everyone looks on as* **Esther** *scrambles onto the floor and tries in vain to put the torn-up picture back together. She gives up.*

Esther   I was helping you.

Joy   Morgan asked me, because I like art. Because I used to be . . . because I wanted to do . . . painting. You took over.

Esther   No . . .

Joy   It's what you do. What you've always done. That's why . . . I can't forgive you.

Esther   Forgive me? For what?

Joy   The dog.

Esther   What dog?

Joy   Phoebe, of course. Phoebe dog! (*A beat/to the others.*) Years back, I used to look after my neighbour's dog. Mrs Williams was an old lady and couldn't take Phoebe out for long walks, so I did it.

Anna   That was kind.

Joy   I loved that dog and she loved me. Then one day, Esther got chatting to Mrs Williams. Said the kids wanted a dog and she asked to borrow Phoebe. They walked her every week and started having her overnight. Then Mrs Williams stopped asking me and Phoebe didn't come round any more.

Esther   You could have carried on borrowing her.

Joy   She wouldn't walk to my front door, she used to cry.

Esther   Because you never gave her any treats.

Joy   You gave her so many beefy chews she left a trail of dog sick up the pavement.

Esther   She was old and she liked her food. You starved her!

Joy   But I didn't kill her. Did I, Esther?

Sheila   How did she die?

Joy   Heart attack . . . well, more of an explosion, actually. She was so vast when she went to the vet, they couldn't find her ribs.

Esther   Phoebe wasn't your dog.

Joy   When she was with me, she was mine. One little thing I had, that you didn't.

Esther   I was being nice. I like being nice.

Joy   Well sometimes you have to stop.

Esther   I try hard with you Joy. I try to be considerate.

Joy   Why? Why do you try so hard?

Esther   Because . . . I want you to be okay . . .

Joy   I'm brilliant. I mean fucking look at me!

Esther   I want . . . I want you to like me.

Joy   I do like you.

Esther   You don't show it.

Joy (*a beat*)   I drive us to choir every week, don't I?

Esther   Yeah, you do, Joy.

Joy   There's not a single person around who knows about me. Nobody, except you. You've . . . got my story . . . and I've got yours. So, if I don't like you, who the fucking hell do I like?

Silence.

Ken (*bright*)   I had no idea about any of this. Anyone else?

Morgan   I think we should take a break.

Joy   Nah, let's keep going.

Morgan   Esther?

Esther   Yeah. Okay.

Joy (*to* **Esther**)   Do you want a wipe?

Esther   No . . . thanks.

Joy   Have one! Please . . .

Esther *slowly takes one.*

Anna   What about the backdrop?

Morgan   We'll work something out. Let's get refocussed.

She signals to them all to gather round. They do and she stands before them.

Morgan   In through the nose and out through the mouth.

They breathe collectively.

Morgan   Stretch your arms out, feel the space in the room.

Ken *reaches out and his hand touches* **Sheila**'s.

Ken   Sorry, I didn't mean to . . .

Sheila   I don't mind, Ken.

Ken   Really?

*Donna Summer's 'I Feel Love' starts to play. The rest of the choir continue to do their breathing exercises/warm ups while **Ken** and **Sheila** are in a kind of dream sequence.*

They dance sensually together. When they reach a crescendo, the music fades and they both fall back into the scene.

Morgan   Back into the room. Deep breath in and out. And relax. (*A beat.*) Well done everybody.

Anna   What's your thought about the start of the show?

Morgan   I've decided we're opening with something completely different. No parts, we'll sing in unison.

Esther   But we need to learn the words.

Morgan   You know them.

She goes to her laptop and plays the first few bars of the backing track to Whitney Houston's 'I Wanna Dance With Somebody'.

*They are all delighted and dance around joyfully while singing along. After the first chorus **Morgan** turns off the music.*

Morgan   Happy?

All   Yes!

Paul   You said never!

Anna   What made you change your mind?

Morgan   Er . . . the television company asked for it.

Paul *freezes.*

Joy   They know their shit.

Paul   I thought we weren't doing *The One Show.*

Freddie   Really?

Anna   Why wouldn't we?

Paul   Something Morgan said . . .

Morgan   Maybe you misunderstood.

Esther   You always told us Whitney was too obvious.

Morgan   Sometimes obvious is . . . the . . .

Ken   The obvious choice.

Sheila   You nailed that one, Ken.

Paul   But you hate Whitney.

Morgan   I don't hate anybody.

Paul   Sure you're still of sound mind, Morgan?

Morgan   The producers wanted something fun and poppy and I have to admit this is the perfect opening.

Paul   And the whole choir is singing it? All of us?

Morgan   Yeah. We're a team.

Joy   Like Aston Villa.

Ken   I should mention . . . I've been assigned a new role.

They all look at him, agog.

Paul   Which is?

Ken   Creative Producer.

Morgan   We said Executive Creative Producer.

Ken   We did!

Sheila   Wow!

Anna   Congratulations.

Paul   And what does the Executive Creative Producer do?

Ken   I'm making a short documentary film of the backstage proceedings on the day of the show. The story behind the story. Imagine . . . er . . . Tony Benn's Diaries on film.

They regard him, bemused.

Freddie   Who's Tony Benn?

Joy   He sang that duet with Amy Winehouse.

Morgan   That was somebody else.

Esther   Have you ever made a film before?

Ken   No, but there's a 4K video zoom camera integrated into my mobile phone that I'm going to use. I'm calling the film *The Making of A Star* in honour of our Freddie.

Freddie   That's . . . overwhelming.

Paul   Who's it for, this documentary?

Morgan   Us.

Anna   What a brilliant idea.

Paul   You're still singing though?

Ken   We discussed that. Danger is the two roles might split my focus.

Sheila   But we need you.

Morgan (*to* **Paul**)   With you and Freddie, the tenors are probably our strongest section. So . . . I think it'll be fine.

Esther   Course it will.

Morgan   It's important to have this record. For archive purposes. And we know we can trust Ken to make it memorable.

Ken   I'll do my best.

Paul   Don't you want to sing?

Ken   I'm not bothered.

Morgan   He's not bothered.

Paul   I need to talk to you, Morgan.

Morgan   We have got quite a lot to get through.

Paul   It's not a request!

Morgan   Okay. (*A beat.*) Why don't you go over your words in the bar, I'll message you once we're done. Anna, can Freddie use your phone for 'Nothing Compares to You'?

Anna   Absolutely. Here.

She hands **Freddie** *her phone.*

The choir head out, singing Whitney Houston.

Ken *remains and overtly starts videoing* **Morgan** *and* **Paul** *on his phone.*

Morgan   You can leave the filming until tomorrow, Ken.

He heads out. **Morgan** *types on her laptop.*

Morgan   Say what you have to say. And then let's move on.

Paul   Move on?

Morgan   Yes.

Paul   Even my close friend in whom I trusted, who ate my bread, has lifted his heel against me. Psalm 41, verse 9.

Morgan   I don't follow . . .

Paul   Judas Iscariot! He's the reason they put 11 icing balls on a simnel cake. 11 not 12. Because he betrayed the Messiah.

Morgan   Ken is not the Messiah.

Paul   You know he chucked the pieces of silver away and hanged himself. And don't think I'm coming to cut you down.

Morgan   I won't be hanging myself.

Paul   What a shame.

Morgan   Do not think for one second that this hasn't been tough for me.

Paul   Funny how you make it look effortless.

Morgan   I have to think of everyone.

Paul   Ken is everyone.

Morgan   I sent the producers a long message explaining why he's important and what the choir is about, they didn't even open the email. Then I spoke to some researcher who said they had another choir ready to go if we dropped out.

Paul   Fuck it, call their bluff.

Morgan   I can't risk them pulling us Paul. I've weighed it up and the best thing to do is carry on.

Paul   It's wrong!

Morgan   You think I didn't fight for him?

Paul *shrugs.*

Morgan   Why do this lot come to this shitty room? Because . . . they don't have anywhere else and this is the best they can do. This group keeps going because I show up week after week. I lug the equipment back and forth, I do the arrangements that people forget and end up singing the tune to, I make sure there are no images of genitalia on the WhatsApp and I take the calls after midnight when there's a queue for The Samaritans. These are my choir members, and they matter to me. (*A beat.*) It would be wrong to pass up this opportunity, after all the work they've done. You've seen them, fizzing with excitement! Plus, Ken doesn't mind.

Paul   You do what you like, I'm no part of this.

Morgan   How come you're suddenly rooting for the underdog? All those times you've complained . . . Ken's boring, Joy's strange, Sheila needs to be sectioned . . .

Paul   That's just nonsense . . . chatter.

Morgan   You've been bitching about them since the beginning. You're so embarrassed you won't even let them speak to James. Why do you even come?

Paul   You asked me.

Morgan   I suppose it can't hurt to be told how fabulous you are. On repeat.

Paul   I might be an arrogant bastard but I would never let them down. Especially not Ken.

Morgan   So you want me to take this away from him? This experience, where he can do something, be part of something. If it doesn't happen, they are all going to be gutted. You know they are.

Paul *takes this in.*

Morgan   One performance to launch us. Once we've had the coverage, a few bookings will start coming in, I'm not imagining a huge triumph, simply a morsel, a taste of better things. And after that, Ken'll be with us again, where he belongs.

Paul   You're not thinking straight.

Morgan   Our best thinking turned us into a wedding band, Paul. I'm learning how to do this, how to be strategic. We thought if we were brilliant and talented we'd make it. But we didn't get chosen. This time we have been. Because I wasn't waiting for someone to find us. I answered an ad and I sold what we do and that's why this is our moment.

Paul   We didn't make it because we weren't good enough.

Morgan   We were. We fucking were.

Paul   We didn't have it. We did not have it.

Morgan   I'm sick of failing, Paul. Of keeping going and making do and being grateful for what I've got. I want it to be my turn to be special.

Paul   Stop . . .

Morgan   Don't you want James to watch you on the television? First time he'll see you singing live, isn't it? Once he hears you, he'll fall head over heels because that is what your voice does to people.

Paul   You think I'm that shallow?

Morgan   Paul, you're not shallow, you're as desperate as the rest of us. (*A beat.*) Don't pretend it doesn't hurt when people not as talented as you start to fly.

Paul   I don't care any more.

Morgan   This way everyone will see us. Hear us.

Paul   It's *The One Show*.

Morgan   Don't you want a glimmer of possibility? Something that isn't this day and tomorrow and every other fucking day that you know is coming. To believe that there's still magic out there for us, some unknown magic . . .

Paul   Not like this.

Morgan   Doesn't matter how it comes. (*A beat.*) I miss it. Don't you miss it? And I'm so lonely. Aren't you so lonely?

Paul (*a beat*)   Yeah.

Silence.

Paul   And what about Freddie?

Morgan   Exactly . . . Freddie is exactly the point . . . we're going to make sure he gets the chances we never had.

Paul   No. This is you, right at the bottom of the barrel.

Morgan *shakes her head.*

Morgan   We are offering something . . . new.

Paul   A new take to help us to understand old things?

Morgan   Yes.

Paul And what if it's all been said before?

Morgan It hasn't. Not by us.

Silence.

Paul You should go back on the dating apps.

Morgan I'm not interested in . . . I'm not like you.

Paul At least I'm willing to take a risk.

Morgan By letting a married man turn you into a lost boy, waiting to be picked for the football team.

Paul Stop . . .

Morgan Yeah, let's stop this . . . stupid talking . . . it's basic shit isn't it . . . this . . . we all just want love, don't we . . . fucking love.

Paul I love you.

Morgan (*a beat*) It's not the kind that matters.

Silence.

Paul Do the right thing by Ken, please?

Morgan I am doing the right thing. (*A beat.*) We could be someone, Paul.

Paul We are someone.

Paul *starts to head to the door.*

Morgan This might be my choir but you're everything to them. You'll break their hearts if you walk. (*A beat.*) I'm calling them back in.

She sends a text.

Morgan So that's it? You're going?

Paul *stops.*

Paul (*a beat*) Where have I got to go?

He takes off his jacket, hangs it up on a hook on the door. The others return with drinks.

Esther   We thought you could do with these.

She hands them a couple of ostentatious cocktails.

Paul   Thanks.

Anna   Cocktails make everything okay.

Joy   The ones with cream in make my bottom explode.

Esther   There's no cream in these.

Joy   I'm just saying.

Morgan *plays 'Nothing Compares to You'.*

Checking **Anna**'s *phone,* **Freddie** *sings the first lines but then stumbles.*

Morgan *stops the music.*

Morgan   We're on tomorrow. You ought to be ready.

Freddie   I am . . . I get a bit . . . you know, when it's a solo . . .

Morgan   Put that nervous energy into the song. Everyone into position.

They start to move when suddenly **Anna**'s *phone beeps continuously.* **Freddie** *looks down at it, he's about to give it to her but stops as he reads.*

Freddie   The pasta was cold and you forgot to take the bathroom bin out, you are the worst mother on the fucking planet and a disgusting bitch . . .

Silence.

Anna   Can I have my phone back please?

All eyes are on her.

Esther   Who sent you that?

Anna   My phone!

He hands it to her. It continues to beep.

Morgan   Anna . . .

Embarrassed, **Anna** *gathers her stuff and hurries out.* **Esther** *starts to go after her.*

Morgan   Leave her . . .

Esther *pauses.*

Morgan   I'll call her later.

Joy   I fancy some fresh air.

Sheila   And me.

They all head out until it's just **Morgan** *and* **Ken.**

Ken   Poor Anna.

Morgan   Yes.

Ken   Do you know much about her?

Morgan *shakes her head.*

Ken   What can we do?

Morgan   Probably nothing.

Ken   Doesn't seem right.

Morgan   It's not. I guess . . . we should try and concentrate on what we're in control of. Big day tomorrow.

Ken   The biggest.

Morgan *nods.*

Ken   Bet you're glad you're not singing those songs about being dead any more.

Morgan   They weren't so bad.

Ken   Now, you're doing Whitney. You've finally arrived!

Morgan   Yes.

Ken   I am pleased. About being Executive Creative Producer.

Morgan   You should be.

Ken (*a beat*)   But I am hurt.

Morgan *takes this in.* **Ken** *smiles gently before he turns and leaves.* **Morgan** *is left alone.*

The choir sing 'Hotel California' as the lights go down.

Scene Four – The day of the concert

Darkness. The One Show *music. A blaze of lights.*

Various researchers and runners/assistants swarm into the space. They are setting up lights, cameras and a catering table.

Spotlight on **Esther**. *A researcher holds out a microphone in front of her.*

Esther   I've been coming since the beginning . . . I work in a supermarket . . . no, I've never had cancer . . . er, none of my children have had it either . . . is that alright? My son gets a terrible rash if he eats pineapple. Does that help? . . . Oh, the choir's changed my life . . . I don't really know how . . .

She retreats and **Joy** *takes her place.*

Joy   Joy.

She looks around awkwardly. She's overwhelmed and can't speak.

Joy   I need the toilet.

She retreats and **Paul** *takes her place, he moves around trying to give the camera his best side.*

Paul   They describe me as the lead singer but that's a label I refute. I'm much more content as a tiny cog serving the big machine . . . Well of course, I do perform most of the solos . . .

Sheila *comes over, takes his position.*

Sheila   I come to choir every week. No . . . my mother died in an armed robbery, before I was born . . . I did have a husband but then, he went missing . . .

Sheila *and the television crew leave the stage. Lights go up.*

Morgan *anxiously flits around tidying, moving chairs, getting the space ready.*

Paul *and* **Freddie** *are going over dropbox on headphones.*

Ken *is filming randomly.*

Joy *and* **Esther** *are painting another canvas.*

Esther   You don't think it's too . . . sentimental?

Joy   I don't fucking care if it is.

Esther   Who said it again?

Joy   Muhammed Ali.

Esther   Should we write his name?

Joy   Won't fit.

Esther   I'll draw a boxing glove.

Joy   Nice.

Esther   Thanks.

Joy   For what?

Esther   I dunno. (*Draws.*)

Joy   It's funny, you do so much for everybody but you're the one who needs the most love.

Esther (*moved*)   Joy . . .

Joy   En silence, mon amie!

They continue painting.

Morgan   Ready everyone?

They all take off their tops to reveal matching T-shirts, emblazoned with 'The Morgan Jackson People's Choir.' **Morgan** *does her best to admire them for a second.*

Morgan   We're lucky the printing company could fit us in last minute. Turn around.

They turn around to reveal their names on the back of the T-shirts. **Ken**'s *top says STAG.*

Morgan *joins* **Paul** *and* **Freddie** *who starts 'Nothing Compares'. He quickly falters.*

Morgan   You should know the lyrics by now!

Freddie   I know them!

Morgan   So what's wrong?

Freddie   The words won't come. They won't . . .

Agitated, he finds his knitting. Starts to knit. He turns away from the audience and sings.

Paul   What are you doing?

Freddie   It's a balaclava.

He sings the first verse of the song, all the while knitting. **Morgan** *takes the knitting from him and throws it on the floor.* **Freddie** *stops singing.*

Morgan   You can't knit in front of the audience.

Freddie   Then I can't sing.

Morgan   But you want to be a singer.

Freddie   I know, I'm a disappointment.

Morgan   You were completely fine in your lessons.

Freddie   It was just you and me.

Morgan   People are coming to watch you. We're raising thousands so you can become a singer.

Freddie   That's what I want, more than anything in the universe. But I can only do it as long as I'm allowed to . . .

He picks up the knitting.

Morgan   If you want it more than anything, you have to be prepared to do anything.

Freddie   I'm trying but . . .

He shakes his head.

Morgan   This is not supposed to be happening! We are sold out! For fuck's sake, Freddie, you fucking fuck!

She goes to shake him, **Paul** *gets in the middle and pulls her off.*

Paul   Get off, Morgan!

Esther *puts her arm around* **Morgan***, pulls her away.*

Paul   Give me a minute with him.

Morgan (*to* **Freddie**)   I'm sorry, I shouldn't have said that . . . I didn't mean it.

Freddie   Don't worry. You've done all this for me, and I'm just . . .

Paul *positions himself opposite* **Freddie***.*

Paul   You lot go . . . go!

He shoos the others away. They retreat to the side, leaving **Paul** *and* **Freddie** *together.*

Freddie   I've let everyone down.

Paul   Shut up.

He indicates they should sit down. They do.

Paul   You know how people say stuff about you, like you're a fantastic singer.

Freddie   Yeah.

Paul   People used to say the same about me. Only I wasn't fantastic. I was one of the best. Much much better than you.

Freddie   And?

Paul   And, whatever happens, if you win some crappy talent show or even a Grammy, you will never touch me.

Freddie   Why are you saying that?

Paul   Because it's true. (*A beat.*) Don't like it, do you? (*He laughs.*) So, there is something more to the hollow prince.

Freddie   Leave me alone.

Paul   What are you going to do? Cancel me?

Freddie   What?

Paul   Well you can't. I'm queer and my sister works in Asda. I'm uncancellable.

Freddie   I don't have a problem with you. I don't have a problem with anybody.

Paul   You should have a problem with a bastard like me. You should have a problem with everything and everybody. You should be raging.

Freddie   Against what?

Paul   The whole thing.

Freddie   How is this going to stop me knitting?

Paul   I don't care about that. Nobody cares about that. Your problem is . . . you think you're it.

Freddie   Me?

Paul   You can't stop thinking about how you sound. Is anybody even listening? Do they know I dropped a baby? And while your brain is whirring around, you are not doing your job which is to share every single second with them. (*Points at audience.*) You've abandoned them when you should be feeling their every breath. An audience doesn't care about the past, they want to forget. They come so they can be with you, in this moment, so every single thing that isn't now has to be dead to you. Or do you want to be stuck in an ensuite singing into your mum's deodorant in front of an Ikea mirror?

Freddie *shakes his head.*

Paul   Then, let them have you. And let them make you . . . magnificent.

Freddie   What about the knitting?

Paul   Unless you know any terrorists, start on a jumper. And . . .

He looks **Freddie** *up and down.*

Paul   . . . get some better clothes.

Freddie   Paul . . .

Paul   What?

Freddie   You should sing it. You'd tear it apart.

Paul   Probably.

Freddie   Please, I want you to.

Silence.

Paul   No. (*A beat.*) I reckon it's time for a new take.

Paul *goes to the laptop, plays the music for 'Nothing Compares'.*

Freddie *starts to sing.* **Morgan** *and the others gather. He knits but slowly drops the needles. He sounds amazing and is emotional and heartfelt. Comes to an end.*

Morgan   You are sensational, Freddie. And this . . . today . . . is going to launch you, so high.

Esther   We could turn the balaclava into a story . . .

Morgan   Yes, we could . . .

Ken   What if he makes it during the show and puts it on during the encore!

Joy   No, Ken.

Morgan   We'll work something out. Thank you, Paul. (*Checks watch.*) Some housekeeping for you . . .

Esther   Wait, Sheila's not here.

Freddie   Or Anna.

Morgan   I'll fill them in. The production crew will be back shortly. Music will be playing from my laptop but via their speakers. We'll let the audience in about ten minutes before we start, they'll go into the bar until we're ready. I will give you a signal. (*She shows them.*) Which means it's time to get into position.

Esther   Gonna be quite a thing, this.

Morgan   More than a thing.

Suddenly **Sheila** *rides in on a bike. She circles around the others.*

Ken   Where did you get that from?

Sheila   My neighbour gave it to me.

Sheila *gets off but is attached to the bike with the lock. She tries to take it off but can't. Others try helping her.*

Sheila   Oh dear, I can't get it away from me.

Joy   Use the key to unlock it.

Sheila   I lost the key, I was in such a rush, it fell down a drain.

Esther   Then it has to be cut off.

Paul   How?

Freddie   That needs a special tool.

Paul   There isn't time.

Sheila   What do I do?

Morgan   Hold on. This is . . . this is my bike . . .

Sheila   Er . . . I don't think so . . .

Morgan   You stole my bike!

Sheila   Oh God, oh my God, my neighbour . . . she's . . . she's a twisted human being.

Morgan   Sheila! I don't care what's wrong with you, you shouldn't have . . . you promised not to do this any more.

Sheila   I am trying.

Ken   She is trying.

Freddie   She's traumatised.

Joy   We're all traumatised.

Morgan   No we aren't! Some of us are functional human beings. I don't steal. I don't tell lies! I don't pretend and make up shit!

Slowly, she falters, turns away from the others.

Sheila   I didn't intend to cause any harm.

Ken   Sheila's just doing her best with what she's got.

Sheila   Once it's off, you can have it back.

*It's as if **Morgan***'s in a daze.*

Sheila   If you want me to go to the police station, I will. They know my name already . . .

Morgan   Never mind. It's okay, Sheila. Just . . . let's leave it.

Joy   Only thing is . . . she's going to have to sing with . . .

She indicates the bike.

Morgan   We'll cover it up.

Ken   I'll zoom in, so it won't feature in *The Making Of A Star*.

Esther   Very thoughtful, Ken.

Freddie   Has anyone heard from Anna?

The choir shake their heads.

Morgan   I sent a couple of messages. But nothing.

Freddie   We could go round her house, check on her.

Morgan   Not appropriate. Plus we won't make it back in time.

Paul   It is getting late.

Morgan   I'll do her part.

Sheila   But I always stand next to Anna.

Paul   You've got the bike for company.

Freddie   What about 'You're All I Need'?

Morgan   I can sing it.

Joy   You?

Morgan   Yeah.

Freddie   Doesn't feel right without her.

Morgan   You have to make it feel right.

Freddie   How?

Morgan   Sing as usual. And trust me . . .

Freddie (*interrupts*)   If she's not here, I can't do it.

Morgan   Of course you can.

Freddie   I mean . . . I won't.

Morgan   Don't be ridiculous.

Freddie *moves away from her.*

Joy   You have to admit, it'll feel different.

Esther   For all of us.

Ken   It will.

Morgan   If somebody's not here, we don't fall apart like a game of Mousetrap. This choir is bigger than that.

Paul   What if we're not?

Morgan   We are, Paul. Everyone here knows we are . . .

Esther   Maybe . . . maybe we don't actually have to do the show. I mean we have raised the money.

Morgan   People are expecting a concert, they haven't given us their money for nothing.

Joy   It's not for nothing, it's to help this . . . young man.

Morgan   We are putting on this concert!

Sheila   To be honest, I don't mind not doing it.

Morgan (*a beat*)   What?

Sheila   I don't mind if the show doesn't happen.

Morgan   But this moment we've arrived at, is the whole . . . point.

Esther   That's one way of looking at it.

Morgan   Are you saying you don't want to do the gig?

Sheila *nods tentatively.*

Morgan   After all the work I've done. We've done.

Sheila   Yes.

Silence as **Morgan** *takes this in.*

Morgan   And . . . is there anybody else who . . . doesn't want to perform?

Slowly they all put their hands up. Stupefied, **Morgan** *sits down.*

Morgan   Because of Anna?

Esther   Not only that.

Morgan   Then why?

Sheila   I just like coming.

Ken   Same.

Joy *nods.*

Morgan   Esther, your family are going to be in the audience. The kids . . .

Esther   They'll never sit still.

Morgan   But this is a chance, your chance . . . to be more.

Joy   More what?

Morgan   Just . . . more . . . (*A beat.*) Don't you all want that?

Ken   I think . . . I'm alright as I am.

Silence.

Freddie   Do you know where she lives?

Morgan *nods.*

Paul   Shall we go? Morgan?

Morgan   James is coming to watch you.

Paul   I told him not to.

Morgan   Why?

Paul   I got tired of waiting to be chosen.

They all look to **Morgan**.

Esther   It's Anna. Our Anna.

Morgan   I don't believe this.

Morgan *gets up, they don't know what she's going to do.*

Morgan   Let's go . . .

As they start to hurry out, **Anna** *appears.*

Anna   I just bumped into Alex Jones.

Joy   You're late.

Anna   Sorry.

She takes her coat off, puts bag down.

Freddie   We thought you weren't coming.

Anna   I wouldn't not come. (*A beat.*) I hope this dress isn't too much. I'm nervous, is anyone else feeling nervous?

Morgan   Anna, we can't pretend we don't know . . .

Anna   I'm not asking anyone to pretend.

Morgan   I have to check that you're okay.

Silence.

Anna   The truth is . . . I'm not who you think I am. I know I look okay and I sound okay. I do lots of okay things in the world. And I definitely seem more okay than all of you. But I'm probably the least okay person here. (*A beat.*) Being here . . . is basically the one thing that makes me happy so when I'm here I don't want to talk about texts or anything else. And I'm not so not okay that I'm going to leave anybody. I like my home, I like it when people admire the bi-folds and the summerhouse. It makes me feel like . . . it makes me feel like someone. I don't want to live in a flat. Have my kids for half a week. (*A beat.*) I know what I'm doing and who I am. I really do. And what I'd like, what I need from you is not to ask me. Can you please not ask me . . .?

Morgan   Are you sure?

Anna   I want to sing. Let's get ready to sing.

Morgan (*a beat*)   Everyone . . . are we happy to continue?

They all nod.

Esther *signals to* **Joy**.

Esther   Joy.

Esther *and* **Joy** *go to the canvas. They turn it around. It says ME WE and has the image of a boxing glove under it.*

Sheila (*like a cat*)   Mewe.

Ken   I'm a cat person.

Esther   It says Me We.

Joy   Muhammed Ali said it. It's . . .

Morgan   The shortest poem in the English language.

Freddie   I like it.

Morgan   It's perfect. Thank you, both of you.

Morgan *glances to the door.*

Morgan   The audience are arriving . . .

They start to go. **Paul** *hangs back. The others look him.*

Ken   Paul?

Paul   I'm frightened.

Esther   But you've done this loads of times.

Paul   Not for years.

Freddie   You'll be okay.

Anna   Come on, there's nothing to be frightened of.

The choir take each other's hands, like a chain. And they lead **Paul** *together.*

A couple of crew return to organise the equipment.

The choir get into their positions on stage.

Morgan   Let's show them what we've got.

A researcher puts headphones on **Morgan**.

Stage management turn on lights.

Ken *is at the side filming.*

Morgan *gets ready to conduct.*

Sound of The One Show *music. The* **Director** *(unseen) speaks via headphones to the* **Presenter** *who also remains unseen. Sound of the* **Director**'*s voice should have a different quality, as if they are in a different space.*

Director *(voiceover)*   Okay, Studio, let's do this thing.

Morgan *checks her headphones, she can hear the director. She looks round, smiles uneasily.*

Morgan   Er . . . excuse me . . . *(To* **Researcher.***)* I can hear him talking to the studio, is that right?

Researcher *urgently indicates that she should keep going.*

Director *(V/O)*   And welcome the choir . . .

Presenter *(V/O)*   Please welcome the Jackson Morgan Community Choir.

Applause. **Morgan** *is concerned at the error. Tries to get the researcher's attention.*

Director *(V/O)*   These are the ones raising the money . . .

Presenter   This choir is singing to raise money for a young man so he can go to college and study music.

Applause.

Presenter   And here's an interview with that very special young man, Frankie!

Unhappy **Morgan** *looks around, she's not sure what to do.*

They play the recorded interview.

Freddie   The best thing about the choir is . . . er . . . it lets people just . . . be. And the people here . . . they make you feel like . . . they're bothered about you. It's made me realise there are still good people . . .

Morgan *goes to her laptop and 'I Wanna Dance With Somebody' starts.*

Ken *starts filming from the front.*

Director (*V/O*)   I thought we told them to cut this guy . . .

Muffled response.

Director (*V/O*)   He's making me feel uneasy. Is anyone else feeling uneasy?

Ken *is getting in the way of the audience's sightline.*

Director (*V/O*)   What the hell is he doing?

Disturbed, **Morgan** *looks at her choir – no* **Ken***,* **Sheila** *attached to a bike. The Me We sign falls down.*

Giggles from the audience.

Director (*V/O*)   Can we get rid of Hannibal Lecter please?

Morgan *pulls out her headphones. Hurls them to the floor.*

Morgan (*shouts*)   Stop!

The choir stop singing. She turns off the music. Bemused silence.

Morgan (*points to* **Ken**) Ken is one of our tenors. (*Finds* **Freddie***.*) And this is Freddie. His name is Freddie.

Unsettled murmurs.

Morgan   And we are The Morgan Jackson People's Choir. We meet every week and we are here because we . . . because we love singing and because . . . we don't sound right without each other.

Morgan *hurriedly takes the iPhone from* **Ken** *and puts him on the stage.*

She goes to the laptop.

Morgan   And this . . . this is who we are.

The Killers 'All These Things That I've Done' starts to play.

She grabs the paint pots that **Joy** *and* **Esther** *were using and chucks paint everywhere. The choir join in and throw paint/use the* *paintbrushes to paint each other. It's utter joyful chaos as if toddlers had been set free.*

Sheila *puts on a balaclava and dances around the stage.*

Freddie *hurls balaclavas out into the audience.*

All the while, the choir sing the song impeccably.

The song comes to an end. It's a scene of mayhem, they are all covered with paint.

Stage management come on and quickly wheel off the lights and cameras.

Joy *takes out her wipes, holds them up triumphantly.*

Each choir member takes one and they wipe each other clean. Lights dim.

Scene Five – Aftermath

The choir clean up the room.

Joy   That was the greatest day of my life.

Esther   Yeah.

Ken *and* **Freddie** *are stacking chairs.* **Sheila** *remains chained to the bike.*

Ken   I still feel giddy.

Freddie   Me too.

Ken   Would you like to come to the cinema with me, Sheila?

Sheila *thinks on this.*

Sheila   No thank you.

Ken   Right.

Sheila   We can do sexual intercourse, though.

Freddie   There's only one thing I feel bad about . . .

Anna   What?

Freddie   Paul didn't get his encore.

Paul   Oh fuck that.

Morgan *is at her laptop.*

Morgan   Who said he didn't?

Music for Primal Scream's 'Movin' on Up' starts to play.

Paul *sings a rapturous version. The choir join in. Convivial joy at the end. Happiness and connection. They are as one.*

THE END.

www.ingramcontent.com/pod-product-compliance
Lightning Source LLC
Chambersburg PA
CBHW041923090426
42741CB00020B/3466